Welcome!

KATHLEEN FINLEY

A Gift to You ____

From ____

Welcome!

Prayers for New and Pregnant Parents

KATHLEEN FINLEY

RESOURCE *Publications* · Eugene, Oregon

Resource Publications
A division of Wipf and Stock Publishers
199 W 8th Ave, Suite 3
Eugene, OR 97401

Welcome!
Prayers for New and Pregnant Parents
By Finley, Kathleen

ISBN 13: 978-1-4982-0461-3
Publication date 9/8/2014
Previously published by Liguori Publications, 2004

To my sons—
Brendan, Sean, Patrick, and Kevin.

You have taught me
and given me
so much life,
as I shared life with you.

Contents

PART V: AT HOME

Introduction

Some events are so naturally holy that everyone involved or around them seems to know how sacred they are; birth and the preparation for birth are clearly in that category.

Whether it's the proverbial cab driver or emergency worker who gets involved in a delivery because the parents didn't make it to the hospital or even the staff in a maternity ward who see the miracle of birth every day, people who are around the process of new life coming to birth seem to know that they are indeed witnessing a miracle.

For all the wonder of pregnancy and birth, we don't often surround this time with much conscious prayer. This book is an attempt to give parents and parents-to-be the opportunity to stop and savor the ways that God is involved in what they are experiencing, from trying to conceive until the child's first birthday. Paradoxically, God is there so powerfully and so closely in the beginning of a new life that it can be easy to miss it at the time.

May this book of prayers be a help to all those who have the privilege of helping bring new life into their families—and into this wonder-filled world.

KATHLEEN FINLEY

O taste and see
that the LORD
is good;
happy are those
who take refuge
in him.

PSALM 34:8

Part I

Before Pregnancy

Prayer for Readiness to Be Parents

Loving God,
who is a beloved parent to us all,
help us both be ready for the privilege of parenthood.

Give us a love of one another
that is ready to take on the challenge
of sharing our lives with another person.
And help us to build a community of support—
friends and family who will be there for us and for our child
when we need their help and advice.

Help us to see that the opportunity to be a parent
may be the closest we'll ever come
to a glimpse of your limitless love for us.
And if it is not your will for us to have a child,
help us to understand other ways in which you are calling us
to give our love generously to others.
Amen

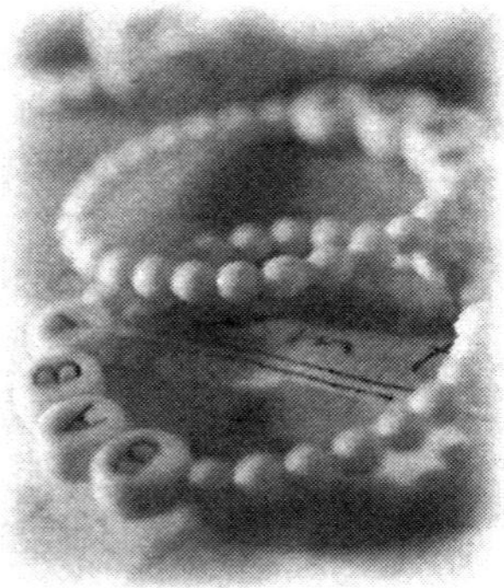

For this reason I bow my knees before the Father, from whom every family in heaven and on earth takes its name. I pray that, according to the riches of his glory, he may grant that you may be strengthened in your inner being with power through his Spirit, and that Christ may dwell in your hearts through faith, as you are being rooted and grounded in love. I pray that you may have the power to comprehend, with all the saints, what is the breadth and length and height and depth, and to know the love of Christ that surpasses knowledge, so that you may be filled with all the fullness of God.

EPHESIANS 3:14–19

Trying to Become Pregnant

Loving God, author of all life,
we long to have a child, if that is your will for us.
As we try to begin a pregnancy,
help us to remember that life is in your hands, not ours,
and that you always have our deepest welfare in mind.

Help us to be patient—even when that is hard—
knowing that you will call us to the responsibility
of being parents when, and if, that is the best way
for us to grow and to know you more deeply.
In the meantime, help us to use our gifts
to help make your world a better place.

Please bless all parents and all those—like us—
who would like to be parents.
Give us the graces to do well *whatever* you call
us to do.
Amen

[Hannah prayed after Samuel's birth:]
"There is no Holy One like the LORD, no one besides you; there is no Rock like our God. . . . The barren has borne seven, but she who has many children is forlorn."
1 SAMUEL 2:2, 5

After a Miscarriage

God of all life, how can this be?
How can you take away this little one
before he or she even had a chance to live?
In faith I know that this creation of yours is with you now,
but I ask for some peace in the midst of my pain
and numbness.

And what is it that you have in mind for me,
as I am left disappointed and without this child,
a little one that I was beginning to prepare to welcome?
Help me to know that you have something
even better in mind for me,
even when I can't imagine it now.

Please bless all those who have lost a child—
either before or after birth;
be with them in their grief and pain,
in their questions and their anger.

Help us to know that you are there
to hold us and to weep with us,
and help us to remember that in your Resurrection
there is always life from death.

Help me to listen for your voice in my life
and to know your deep care and peace
as I give this unborn child into your loving arms.
Amen

Then was fulfilled what had been spoken through the prophet Jeremiah:

> ***"A voice was heard in Ramah,***
> ***wailing and loud lamentation,***
> ***Rachel weeping for her children;***
> ***she refused to be consoled,***
> ***because they are no more."***

MATTHEW 2:17–18

Part II

During Pregnancy

Blessing for a Pregnant Mother

(If this blessing is done by someone other than the mother, that person should place a hand on the mother's stomach—or on her shoulder, if that is more comfortable for her. If the mother is saying this prayer alone, she should place her hands on her stomach and change the wording as needed.)

God, who is both mother and father to us,
bless this new mother and the child now growing within her.
Help her to carry this child safely,
growing each day in love for her child.
Give her good health
and help her to make good choices about her rest and care,
about what she feeds herself and this new life she nourishes.
Give her the help and support she needs
as she shares her body so intimately
and allows this child to mature within her.

Give her grace and guidance during this important time;
help her to see how naturally contemplative that time is,
as she is reminded to look inward by the child's movements,
to see her own goodness and her ability to share life.
Help her to know your love for her more deeply during this time—
a love and care that surrounds her,
just as her womb surrounds her child.
Amen

> ***Now the birth of Jesus the Messiah took place in this way. When his mother Mary had been engaged to Joseph, but before they lived together, she was found to be with child from the Holy Spirit.***
>
> **MATTHEW 1:18**

Blessing for an Expectant Father

(If this blessing is done by someone other than the father, that person should place a hand on his shoulder. If the father is saying this prayer alone, he should place his hands open before him and change the wording as needed.)

Father of love,
bless this father
as he and his wife journey through
the process of pregnancy together
and prepare to bring a child into this world.

Give him the graces and blessings he needs
to be a support to his wife
as she experiences all the changes of these months.

Help him to begin to imagine and love this little person—
an even harder process for him than for the mother
because he doesn't experience the inner changes that she does.

Help him to know your deep love—
a love that waits expectantly for, and delights in, each of us—
as he now waits for this child to be born.

Give him the grace to be a powerful image
of your strong yet tender love for this child,
and give him all the gifts that he will need
to share his faith with this new life
growing within his wife.
Amen

See what love the Father has given us, that we should be called children of God; and that is what we are.

1 John 3:1

Blessing for a Stepparent

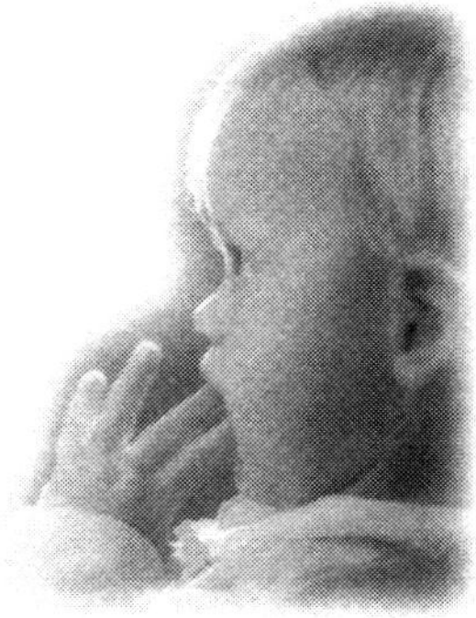

Tender God,
bless this parent whose bond with this child
is one of love, not of blood.
Give this parent all the wisdom that is needed
to be a faithful presence of love in this child's life—
not taking the place of the biological parent,
but being an extra source and reflection
of your love for this child.

Please give this parent special graces
for the difficult challenges that may lie ahead;
give abundantly of your care, patience, and acceptance
so that she or he may be a source
of those qualities in this child's life
and to help this child to know
that there are no limits and exclusions to real love.
Amen

Love is patient; love is kind; love is not envious or boastful or arrogant or rude. It does not insist on its own way; it is not irritable or resentful; it does not rejoice in wrongdoing, but rejoices in the truth. It bears all things, believes all things, hopes all things, endures all things. Love never ends.

1 Corinthians 13:4–8

Blessing for a Single Mother

(If this blessing is done by someone other than the mother, that person should place a hand on the mother. If she is saying this prayer alone, she should pray with her hands open before her and change the wording as needed.)

God, who knows the future of us all,
bless this woman as she faces
the prospect of motherhood alone.
Give her all the graces and wisdom she will need
to make good choices for her child and for her own life.
Help her to weigh the prospect of adoption,
if that is appropriate.
And help her to know the support and care
she has from others,
as well as your deep love.
Give her the strength and courage
to love this child well;
hold her close to you and wrap her in your love.
Amen

O LORD, you have searched me and known me.
You know when I sit down and when I rise up;
you discern my thoughts from far away. . . .
Even before a word is on my tongue,
O LORD, you know it completely.
You hem me in, behind and before,
and lay your hand upon me.
Such knowledge is too wonderful for me;
it is so high that I cannot attain it.

PSALM 139:1–2, 4–6

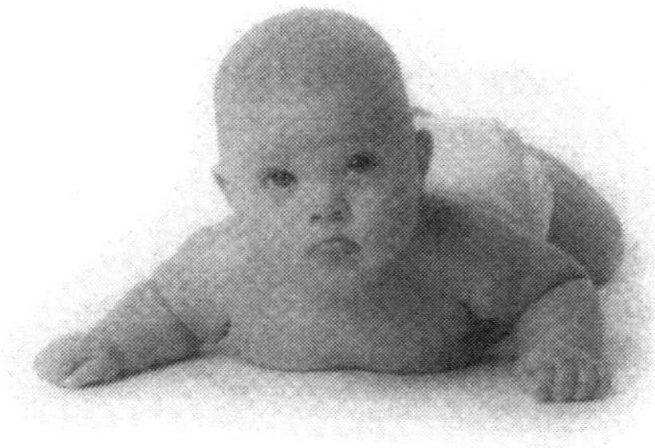

Prayer for an Uninvolved Father

Tender God, who delights in each one of us,
I pray for this father who does not yet understand
his involvement in this pregnancy.

Help him to know the privilege and the responsibility
to which he has been called,
and turn his heart toward the needs of the mother
and his growing child.
Help him imagine the wonder of a little one calling him "Daddy"
and of scooping up an infant
and snuggling a tiny person to his cheek.

Loving God, who commands the winds and the seas,
please begin to help shape this man into a loving father.
Amen

[Mary's] husband Joseph, being a righteous man and unwilling to expose her to public disgrace, planned to dismiss her quietly. But just when he had resolved to do this, an angel of the Lord appeared to him in a dream and said, "Joseph, son of David, do not be afraid to take Mary as your wife, for the child conceived in her is from the Holy Spirit."

MATTHEW 1:19–20

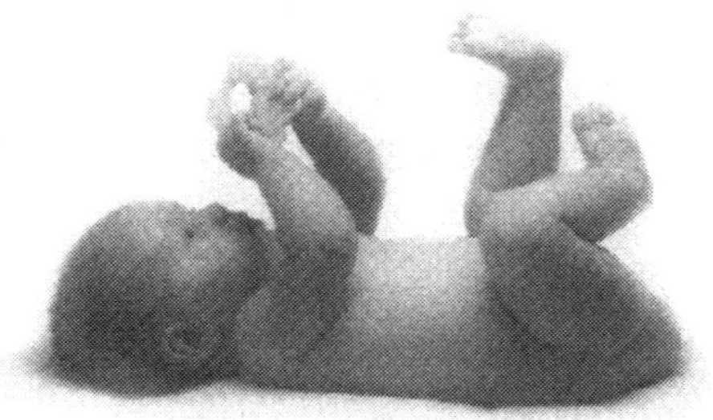

Worries and Concerns During Pregnancy

God of all life,
sometimes I worry about this pregnancy,
about whether this child is developing normally,
whether there will be any complications at birth
or any genetic conditions or other health problems
after this child is born.

In the midst of these and other concerns,
help me to know
that you are holding this little one close to you
and that you will give me all the strength to handle
whatever the future holds for this child.

Jesus, you told the father of a boy who was possessed
that everything is possible to one who trusts.
Help me to trust that you,
the source of this new little life that is growing right now,
will bring this child to the end for which you intend.
Amen

Are not two sparrows sold for a penny? Yet not one of them will fall to the ground apart from your Father. . . . So do not be afraid; you are of more value than many sparrows.
MATTHEW 10:29–31

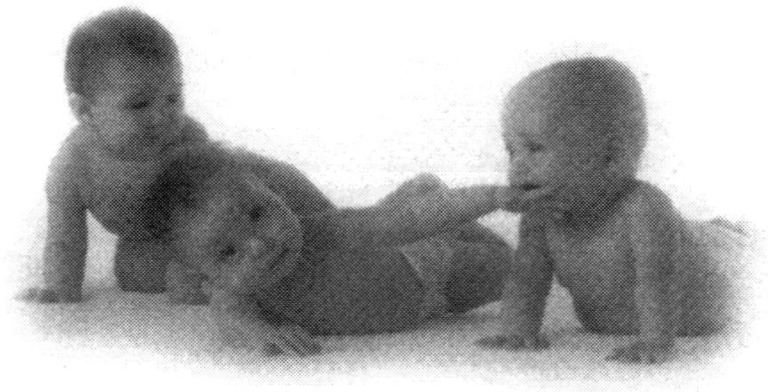

For a Pregnancy That Isn't the First Time

Generous God,
we are pregnant again,
and again we ask your blessings on this child,
who is developing and growing toward birth.

We also ask your blessings and grace on us as parents
and on the sibling(s) this child already has.

Help us to be a source of love and acceptance
for this little one,
to be all that he or she will need
to be able to know your love more fully.

Help us to delight in this child,
as we have delighted in the child(ren)
we already have,
and help us to be patient and open to him or her,
remembering that each child is unique
and, first and last, is yours,
only on loan to us.
Amen

But Zion said, "The LORD has forsaken me,
my Lord has forgotten me."
Can a woman forget her nursing child,
or show no compassion for the child of her womb?
Even these may forget,
yet I will not forget you.
See, I have inscribed you on the palms of my hands;
your walls are continually before me.

ISAIAH 49:14–16

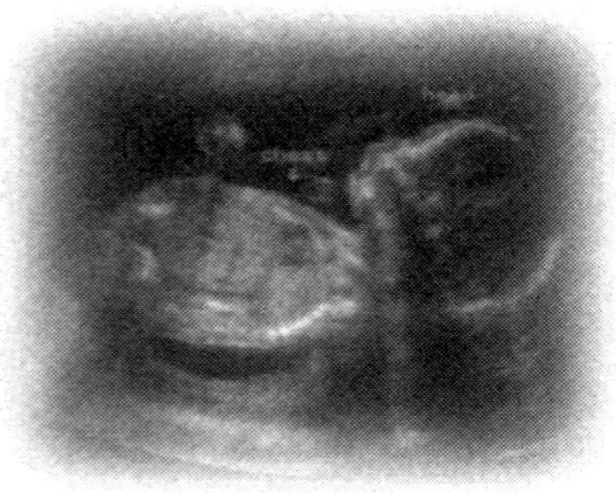

After an Ultrasound and Hearing the Baby's Heartbeat

God of every beat of our hearts,
thank you for the amazing miracle of life,
the proof of which we have just seen (and heard).
You are, indeed, an awesome God,
who shares life with us
in an incredibly complex and lavish way.

How can we thank you enough
for the privilege of living in a time
when we can see and hear *inside* the womb
and know more fully the miracle
that is unfolding within the child's mother?

We ask now for the grace
to also have the sense of wonder and appreciation
that we have today when we most need it:
at the times when caring for this child
may become difficult and challenging.

Help us to remember even then
how incredibly complex this little one is
and that you have made this being in your own image.

And please give us all the gifts that we need
to help this little one grow to be someone
who continues to give you both delight and praise.
Amen

For it was you who formed my inmost parts;
you knit me together in my mother's womb.
I praise you, for I am fearfully and wonderfully made.
Wonderful are your works;
that I know very well.
My frame was not hidden from you,
when I was being made in secret,
intricately woven in the depths of the earth.

PSALM 139:13–15

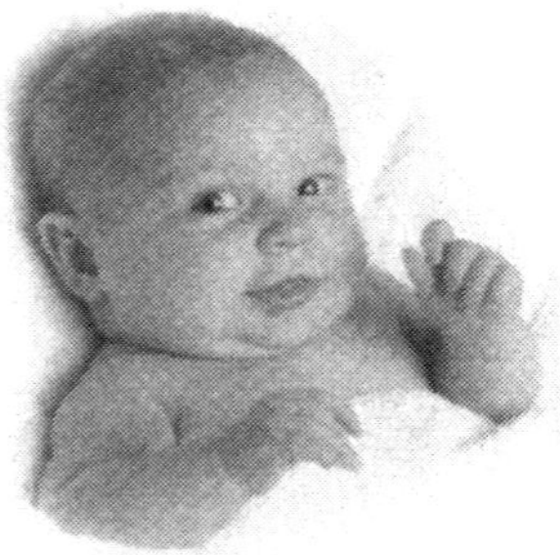

On Feeling the Baby Move

God of all the living
and the source of every move we make,
thank you for the experience
of feeling this little one move within me.

I keep trying to imagine this child inside my body,
but it has been so hard to picture
this tiny one as a separate person yet.

That task is now a bit easier,
because the moment I just felt
was clearly not caused by me.

As the months go on—no matter what I am doing—
when I feel the baby kick and move inside me,
help me to remember, as I focus my attention inward,

to be more aware of all that you are accomplishing
within me and to be grateful for the
privilege of sharing life with this new little person.

Please help this child to be healthy
and to use all his or her strength
and energy to praise you.
Amen

When Elizabeth heard Mary's greeting, the child leaped in her womb. And Elizabeth was filled with the Holy Spirit and exclaimed with a loud cry, "Blessed are you among women, and blessed is the fruit of your womb. And why has this happened to me, that the mother of my Lord comes to me? For as soon as I heard the sound of your greeting, the child in my womb leaped for joy. And blessed is she who believed that there would be a fulfillment of what was spoken to her by the Lord."

LUKE 1:41–45

On Hearing the News of a Multiple Pregnancy

God of wonders and surprises,
you've certainly surprised us this time.
When we heard that we were to have more
than one child,
it brought up all kinds of feelings for us.

Besides the obvious delight,
there is also concerns about our children's health
and the health of their mother,
the increased demands on our resources
and our time,
as well as wondering about their relationship
with each other.

Help us to remember
that *all* these things are in your hands—
just as our children are,
even now in their mother's womb—

and that you will give us all that we need
to care for them well, during this pregnancy and after.

Bless them and us;
help them to know that they are *each* special
and precious in our eyes—and in yours.
Amen

Isaac prayed to the LORD for his wife, because she [Rebekah] was barren; and the LORD granted his prayer, and his wife Rebekah conceived. The children struggled together within her; and she said, "If it is to be this way, why do I live?" So she went to inquire of the LORD. And the LORD said to her,

"Two nations are in your womb,
and two peoples born of you shall be divided;
the one shall be stronger than the other,
the elder shall serve the younger."

When her time to give birth was at hand, there were twins in her womb.

GENESIS 25:21–24

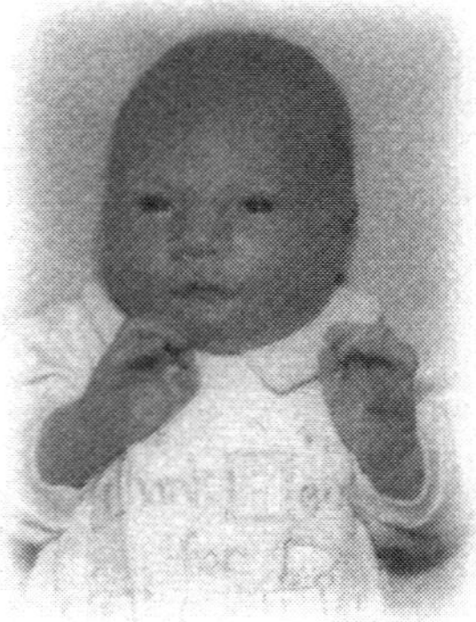

In the Midst of Morning Sickness

Gentle God,
this part of the experience of pregnancy isn't easy.
It's hard to have an unsettled stomach
and at times to not be hungry for much
or not be able to keep food down very easily.

Help me to remember
that what is happening within me—
at least, in part—
is a kind of motion sickness.
There is so much growth and activity
happening inside me
that's it's hard for my body
to keep up with all the new life that is happening.

Give me the strength and the patience
that I need to get through this time,
knowing that you are doing amazing things within my
body and that growth is not usually easy.

(And when I think about what Jesus underwent
to give *us* the fullness of life,
my sacrifice somehow doesn't look so hard.)

Please bless all those who are sick—
whether because of pregnancy or other reasons.
Give them someone to care for them
and a knowledge that you are there,
suffering with them.

And thank you for this busy life within me,
growing to fullness in your love.
Amen

> ***As the sun was setting, all those who had any who were sick with various kinds of diseases brought them to him [Jesus]; and he laid his hands on each of them and cured them.***
>
> **LUKE 4:40**

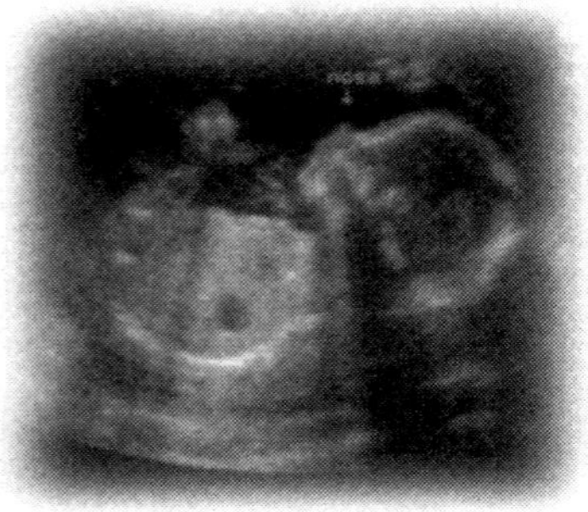

Anointing the Baby in Utero

(Anointing is an ancient practice of asking God to bless someone while placing oil on that person's skin; it is used in the sacraments of baptism, confirmation, holy orders, and the anointing of the sick. Although the child can't be anointed directly, this prayer can be an opportunity for the parents and others to ask God to bless this developing infant. The mother's abdomen should be available to bless and any kind of oil may be used here—mineral oil, baby oil, or other scented oils.)

Tender God,
we ask your special blessing on this infant
now growing within this mother.
Keep this little one in your care,
and help us to remember
that this child is held in your love
as well as ours.

As this wee person prepares for birth,
prepare us, too, to be a family
that can welcome this tiny gift
and to be a sign of your love in his or her life.
We now bless this child with oil.

(Each person present can make the sign of the cross with oil.)

In the name of the Father, and of the Son,
and of the Holy Spirit,
and we ask you, as the Trinity, to hold this child
close to you until the day that we can.
Amen

"Before I formed you in the womb I knew you, and before you were born I consecrated you; I appointed you a prophet to the nations."
JEREMIAH 1:5

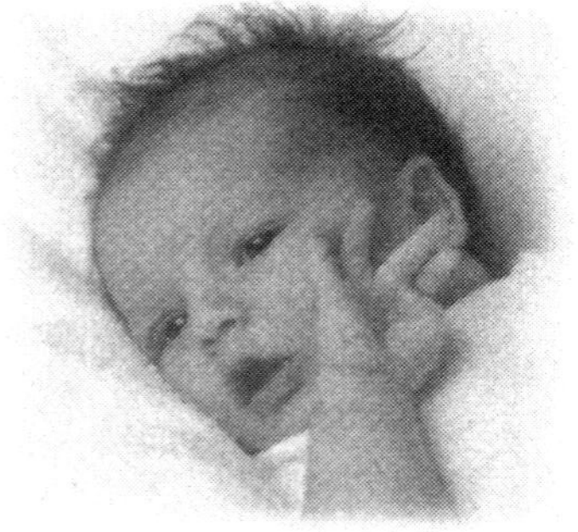

After Taking a Childbirth Class

God of all knowledge,
thank you for the opportunity we have
to learn about the amazing process of birth.

As we prepare for this child's birth,
help us also be aware of the miracle of each of our births
and to be grateful for all
that our parents have done for us.

Please bless the instructor
and bless all the other parents taking this class;
be with them to help them know your peace
as they prepare for this important time in their lives.

Help us to remember that,
along with the skills that we are learning
and the equipment and the professionals
that will be helping us,
your love will be with us every step of the way.

During this time of preparation
please bring to "birth" in us
a new appreciation for the wonder of life
and of your unending delight in each of us.
Amen

Teach me your way, O LORD,
that I may walk in your truth;
give me an undivided heart to revere your name.
I give thanks to you, O Lord my God, with my whole heart,
and I will glorify your name forever.
PSALM 86:11–12

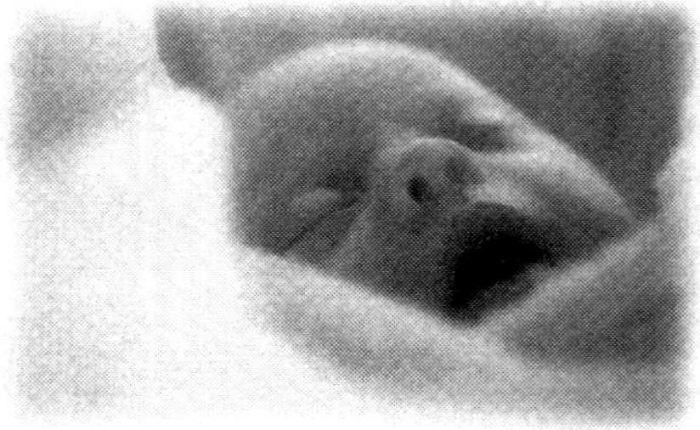

Choosing a Name for the New Baby

Loving God of all,
help us in the important task of naming this child.
Give us wisdom to know the name
that would be best for this new little person
soon to come into our lives.

Help us to weigh and choose well,
knowing that this little one will have to live
with what we choose throughout her or his life.
Keep us open to new possibilities
that we may not have considered
and open to one another's feelings and preferences.

Whatever name we choose,
help us to always say it lovingly and respectfully—
rarely in anger or frustration—
knowing that each one of us is precious and unique to you.

And help us to remember that your "name"
for each one of us is "precious child."
Amen

But now, thus says the LORD,
he who created you, O Jacob,
he who formed you, O Israel:
Do not fear, for I have redeemed you;
I have called you by name, you are mine.
ISAIAH 43:1

During the Last Phase of Pregnancy

While they were [in Bethlehem], the time came for [Mary] to deliver her child. And she gave birth to her firstborn son.

Luke 2:6–7

God of all life,
the time for this child's birth is drawing near.
Help us wait patiently through these last few weeks,
knowing that the time for this child to appear
is in your hands, not ours.

Help us to prepare in all the practical ways—
getting the bed, the clothes, and the car seat ready
and any other equipment we may need.
But help us, even more, to prepare our hearts
to welcome this new little person
who comes with a special message of love
straight from you.

Prepare us to be the best parents we can
to this new little one and to be open to learn
all that you have to teach us through his or her life.
Amen

For a Pregnancy Past Due Date

Loving God,
we are waiting.
And we're trying to be patient,
but it gets harder as the days go on.

Help us to remember that you are holding all of us—
this new child to be born and us as parents—
in your loving care.

Just as you sent Jesus in the fullness of time,
you will send us this little one when the time is right.
Help us to trust in your goodness and timing,
and prepare our hearts for the many ways
that we will be waiting for this child
throughout his or her life—
whether waiting for him or her to learn the next skill
or to make good choices.

And help us to remember in our waiting
that in your time it's always now.
Amen

For everything there is a season, and a time for every matter under heaven: A time to be born. . . .
ECCLESIASTES 3:1–2

For Complications in Pregnancy

God of love,
be near me at this difficult time.
Help me to know
your comforting presence
and to remember that you
never give me a difficult task
without giving me the gifts to handle it.

Help me to picture myself
in your loving hands,
knowing that you hold me tenderly
and that you will help me
through this difficult time.

Give to me
and the medical professional helping me
the wisdom to do what is best
for this child and for me.

Help me to trust you more each day
and to grow in your love.
Amen

Hear my prayer, O LORD;
let my cry come to you.
Do not hide your face from me
in the day of my distress.
Incline your ear to me;
answer me speedily in the day when I call.
PSALM 102:1–2

Part III

During Labor & Delivery

Blessing for the Birth Coach

Loving God, who brings all things to birth,
bless this birth coach as he/she prepares
to help with the important job of assisting
with this labor and delivery.

Give this coach all the energy, graces,
and wisdom necessary to help this mother effectively,
including empathy for her,
patience when needed,
an awareness of how to comfort and encourage her,
and the ability to help keep her focused.

Help all who assist in this birth
to do so with wisdom and competence
and help them to be aware of the wonder of this time
and to see your goodness in the miracle of life as it unfolds.

Thank you for all the ways
that you have been present during this pregnancy;
please help bring this child to birth safely.
Amen

Yet it was you who took me from the womb; you kept me safe on my mother's breast. On you I was cast from my birth, and since my mother bore me you have been my God.

PSALM 22:9–10

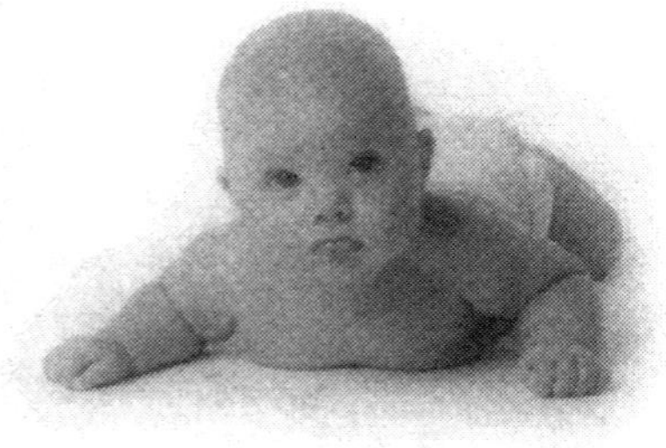

Early in the Process of Labor

God of all beginnings,
be with us now as we launch
into the never-to-be-repeated process
of bringing this unique child to birth.

Help us to remember
that you are with us every step of the way,
watching over us and bringing us
to "birth" as parents,
as well as giving life to this new child
outside the womb.

Give us the patience we need
during this time
and help us to watch for changes
and needs that may arise along the way.
Help us also to be able
to recall this experience later
so that we may tell this child
the story of his or her beginnings.

Thank you for all the ways
you have been with us
through this pregnancy
and for the wonder of this process
through which we each came to be.
Amen

> ***We know that the whole creation has been groaning in labor pains until now; and not only the creation, but we ourselves, who have the first fruits of the Spirit, groan inwardly while we wait for adoption, the redemption of our bodies.***
>
> **ROMANS 8:22–23**

During an Unusually Long Labor

God of my days and nights, I'm getting tired.
This child is taking a long time to come to birth,
and this is really hard on me.
Please help me to remember that, during this time,
you are holding both me and my child very tenderly.

Give me the patience that I need at this point
and help me to remember how long and patiently
you have waited for *me*—
to be aware of you in my life,
to appreciate the goodness and beauty
that you pour into my days,
and to learn to love others
with a bit of the love that you have for me.

Help me to trust
that this birth is happening in your time
and that you are in charge here—

both as surely and as hiddenly
as you are every other day of my life.
Give me your peace and your presence;
with both of those I can make it through
any challenge that you give me.

And help me to remember
that this new little person is clearly worth
waiting for.
Amen

For a long time
I have held my peace,
I have kept still and
restrained myself;
now I will cry out
like a woman in labor,
I will gasp and pant.
Isaiah 42:14

During the Harder Contractions

God of love,
this is difficult.
We're trying to use all the information
that we were taught,
but this part of the labor
is really painful and puzzling.

Be with us through this time
and help us to remember
that a part of any birth is being willing
to let some of the old ideas and expectations die.

Help us to see this time as part of the way
that you call us to die and rise with you every day.
Give us all the strength we need to trust you now,
knowing that the new life of birth is not far away.
Amen

For I heard a cry as of a woman in labor,
anguish as of one bringing forth her first child,
the cry of daughter Zion gasping for breath,
stretching out her hands,
"Woe is me!"

Jeremiah 4:31

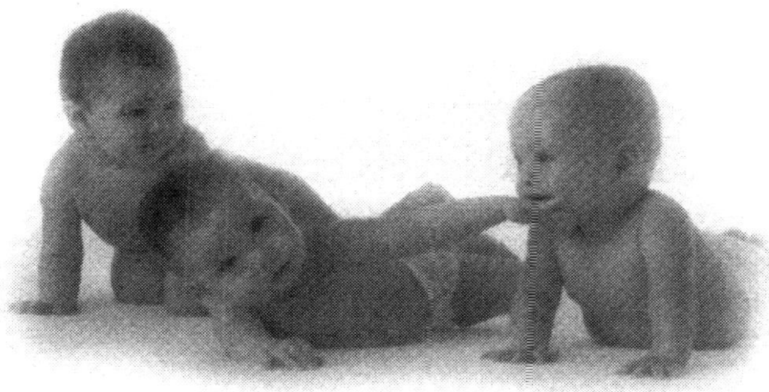

> ***Shall I open the womb and not deliver? says the LORD; shall I, the one who delivers, shut the womb? says your God.***
> **ISAIAH 66:9**

For an Induced Labor

God of all that is,
thank you for the knowledge and ability
that allows these health professionals
to induce my labor.
Please help them to use all their expertise
to make this process go smoothly.

Help me to remember that your time
is not always my time
and that your ways and plans
are often not the same as mine.
Help me to see myself wrapped in your care
as you bring this child to birth in me.

And please bless all those today
who are bringing children to birth
without all the resources that are available for me;
keep them also safely in your care.
Amen

Thanksgiving for a Safe Delivery

God of all life,
thank you for bringing all of us
safely through the process of this birth.
Although births happen every day,
we thank you for the incredible wonder
and complexity of this process.

Thank you for this new little person,
so ready to meet the world and explore it.
Help us to rest now so that, with your help,
we can be ready to take on
the challenges that lie ahead.

Never let us forget the graces of this time,
when so much could have gone wrong,
and instead it went incredibly well.
Help us to remember—
especially when we are tempted to forget—
how much we are always in your hands,
even before we are born.

Amen

When a woman is in labor, she has pain, because her hour has come. But when her child is born, she no longer remembers the anguish because of the joy of having brought a human being into the world.

JOHN 16:21

For a child has been born for us, a son given to us…
Isaiah 9:6

After a Caesarean Delivery

God of surprises,
although this birth ended up differently
than I thought it would,
I'm really glad that the technology exists
that helped keep my baby safe.

Thank you for all the people with their expertise
who helped things go so well.
Although I have more healing in store for me
than from a "normal" birth,
I also have a baby who is safe and healthy.

Watch over us both as we recover from this birth
and get to know each other,
and thank you for your grace,
once again so clearly at work in my life.
Amen

Blessing for the Newborn

God of all life,
we bless and thank you
for the wonder of this new child before us.

From the complexity of her fingers and toes
to the ability to observe what's around her
and to search for nourishment
she is so clearly made in your image and likeness.

You have been forming this little one for many months—
giving her unique fingerprints,
knitting together her bones, nerves, and muscles
and even letting her hear our voices—
and now we are privileged
to see your amazing handiwork in her.

Thank you for the miraculous gift
of this new little person into our lives
and for the privilege of helping her to grow
and to come to know you in her life.

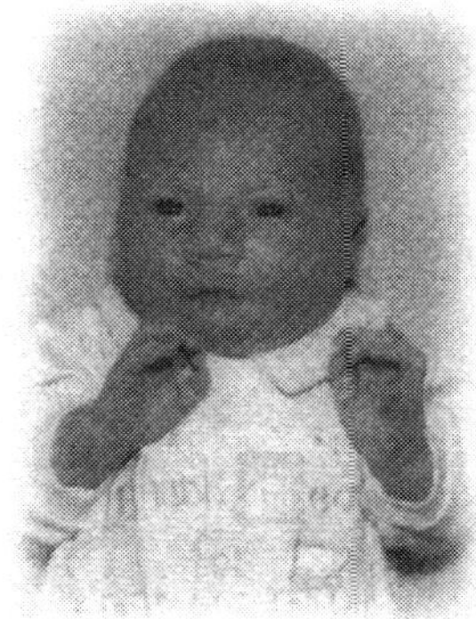

> ***In the time of King Herod, after Jesus was born in Bethlehem of Judea, wise men from the East came to Jerusalem, asking, "Where is the child who has been born king of the Jews? For we observed his star at its rising, and have come to pay him homage."***
>
> **MATTHEW 2:1–2**

Give us all the graces we need
to do this as well as we can—
today and every day of her life and of ours.

(Each person present can trace the sign of the cross on the newborn's forehead.)

We ask you to bless this little one now
and keep her close to you
in the name of the Father, and of the Son,
and of the Holy Spirit.
Amen

Blessing for a Premature Infant

God of all parents,
I guess this little one couldn't wait to be with me
and is here before his time.

Thank you for all the medical resources
that help sustain him
while he grows to be fully ready to survive on his own.
Give me the patience and the gifts I need to cope
with any special complications
that this premature birth may involve.
And give him the clear assurance of my love and yours,
as so many people help him to thrive right now.

Thank you for the many ways in which you always look after us,
especially those most in need of your care.
Bless *(name of child)* now and be with him.
In the name of the Father, and of the Son, and of the Holy Spirit.
*(Each person present can trace the sign of the cross
on the newborn's forehead.)*
Amen

***Protect me, O God,
for in you I take refuge.
I say to the LORD,
"You are my Lord;
I have no good apart
from you."***
PSALM 16:1–2

For Twins or Other Multiple Births

Generous God,
in our role as parents, you have given us
a multitude of blessings with these births.

Please bless these children
and help them to know what a gift
they are to us;

we ask you for all the gifts that we need
to care for these children well
and the wisdom to know when to ask
for the help of others.

Teach us not to prefer one over the other
or to compare them with each other;
help them to be close
and yet healthy, separate individuals.

Give us the grace to continue
to rejoice in the gift of their births;
help us not to get bogged down
in the challenges that they may present.
For this we rely on your help,
as we do every minute of our lives.
Amen

When her time [Rebekah's] to give birth was at hand, there were twins in her womb.
Genesis 25:24

Blessing for a Receiving Blanket and First Clothes

God of love,
we ask your blessing on these clothes
which our new child will wear as we take her home.

Help us to wrap her in our love
as well as in these garments,
just as you wrap us warmly in your tender love.

Help us to appreciate her as a gift
to our family every day of her life
and never to take her for granted.

Give her enough to wear throughout her life
and help her never to be worried
about what she wears
and always able to share what she has with others.

As we wash and use these clothes
and others she will wear,
help us to remember that, as Jesus reminded us,
in caring for those
who are the least of our brothers and sisters,
we are helping to clothe and care for you.
Amen

> ***And she [Mary] gave birth to her firstborn son and wrapped him in bands of cloth, and laid him in a manger, because there was no place for them in the inn.***
>
> **LUKE 2:7**

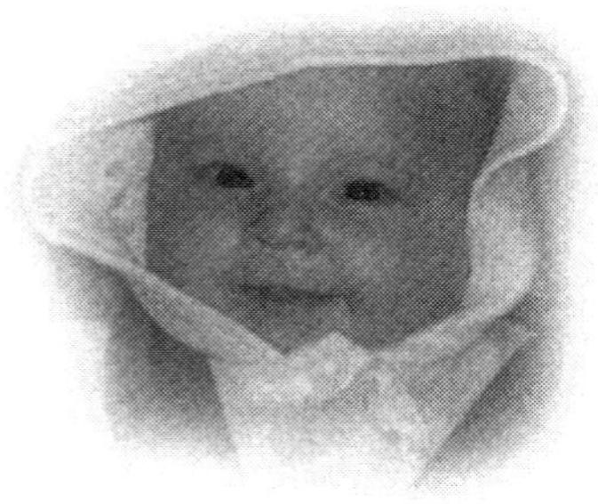

For Visitors at the Hospital

Loving God who welcomes all,
thank you for all those who have come
to see me and the new baby here at the hospital.
Help them to know what a blessing
they already have been in our lives,
and thank you for the support
that they will continue to give us
in the years to come.

Please help to remind me that by their visits
this little one is not only *mine* but *ours*,
already part of a community
of friends and family
that will help to raise this child.

As the years go by,
please continue to bring
a rich set of friends into our lives,
so that they may help us to know your love
by their love and acceptance
and just by being who they are.
Amen

When the angels had left them and gone into heaven, the shepherds said to one another, "Let us go now to Bethlehem and see this thing that has taken place, which the Lord has made known to us." So they went with haste and found Mary and Joseph, and the child lying in the manger.

Luke 2:15–16

Part IV

Adoption

Waiting for Approval for an Adoption

Loving God, this waiting is so hard.
We've done the home study
and filled out so many papers,
and still we wait.
We're trying to be understanding about how long
the processing of this paperwork can take
and yet our arms ache for our child.

Help us to remember that you know how we feel;
you ache for us like this
when we draw away from you and your love,
and you long to have us back in your arms.

Help us to use this time well,
to really prepare our hearts to receive this child
as the true gift that he or she will be.
And give us patience, please, dear God.
Amen

I waited patiently
for the LORD;
he inclined to me
and heard my cry. . . .
He put a new song
in my mouth,
a song of praise
to our God.
Many will see and fear,
and put their trust in
the LORD.

PSALM 40:1, 3

On Hearing News of an Adoptive Child Coming

Alleluia! Our waiting is finally over!
Our child will be coming to us soon.
Help us to accomplish all the last-minute preparations
and handle all the details,
but mostly help us to finish preparing our hearts
for our new son.

Help us to give our new child a home
that will be a place to grow and flourish.
Help us to teach him many things,
but, most importantly, help us to teach him how to love
by the way we try to love him as you have loved us.

Keep us all safe in your love
until we are together as a family.
Amen

The daughter of Pharaoh came down to bathe at the river, while her attendants walked beside the river. She saw the basket among the reeds and sent her maid to bring it. When she opened it, she saw the child. He was crying, and she took pity on him, "This must be one of the Hebrews' children," she said. "When the child grew up... she took him as her son. She named him Moses, "because," she said, "I drew him out of the water."

Exodus 2:5–6, 10

Blessing for the Journey to Meet the Adoptive Child

God of our comings and goings,
we are about to embark on an important trip,
one that will change our lives forever.

Be with us and give us your grace and protection
as we travel to pick up our adopted daughter
and begin our journey together into the future.

Help us to know your presence in a special way
as we all begin a new chapter of our life as a family.

Calm our fears and concerns
and help us to know your deep love
as we learn how to best love each other.
Amen

The LORD will keep you from all evil;
he will keep your life.
The LORD will keep
your going out and your coming in
from this time on and forevermore.
PSALM 121:7–8

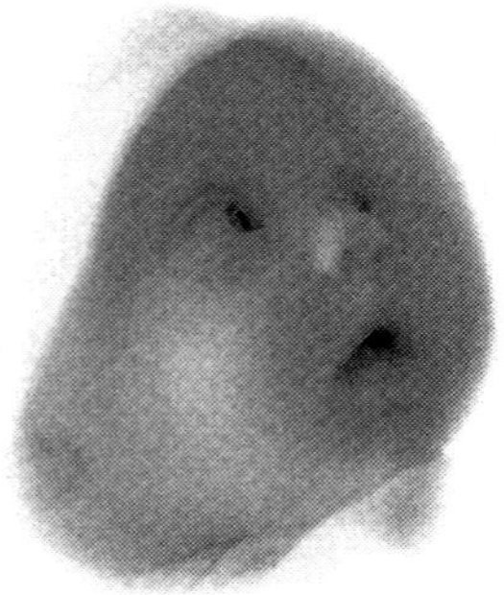

Blessing for an Adopted Child

Loving God,
we ask you to bless this new son of ours,
who is a gift to us in so may ways.

Bless all those who have made his life possible,
including his birth parents
and all those who have cared for him until now.
And please bless those who have made it possible
for him to now be a part of our family.

Keep him in your love and ours always
and help him to know
how much we love him as he grows.
Give us, as parents, all the gifts and wisdom
that we need to raise this child well,
and help us to remember
that he was and is your child first.

(Each person present can trace the sign of the cross on the adopted child's forehead.)

We ask you to bless him and draw him close to you,
in the name of the Father, and of the Son,
and of the Holy Spirit.
Amen

> ***Blessed be the God and Father of our Lord Jesus Christ, who has blessed us in Christ with every spiritual blessing in the heavenly places, as he chose us in Christ before the foundation of the world to be holy and blameless before him in love. He destined us for adoption as his children through Jesus Christ, according to the good pleasure of his will.***
>
> **EPHESIANS 1:3–5**

Thanksgiving Prayer for the Birth Parents

God, who is both mother and father to us,
thank you for the gift that we have been given
through the selflessness of our child's birth parents.
It can't have been an easy decision for them to give her up,
and that decision has changed the lives of many people.

Please be with them and give them comfort,
both now and when they need it in the future—
at the times when they think about this child
and wonder how she is.

Help them to know that we will care for her well
and will help her to always be grateful to them
for the gift of her life.
Please bless her parents richly
and give them all that they need;
they have shared a most precious gift with us.
Amen

With all your heart honor your father,
and do not forget the birth pangs of your mother.
Remember that it was of your parents you were born;
how can you repay what they have given to you?

Sirach 7:27–28

Part V

At Home

On Bringing the New Baby Home

God of all welcomes,
we have brought our son home,
to this place where he can grow and thrive.
Help our home to be a place
filled with many good memories for him,
a place that echoes with love and joy.

We ask that you give to this house
and to our family abundant peace
and an ability to forgive and heal wholeheartedly
all the many ways in which we may hurt one another.

Give us the graces we need
in the coming days and months to adjust
to the changes our new son will bring into our lives
and help him to know by our care for him
what a delight he is in this family.
Amen

Then he [Jesus] went down with them and came to Nazareth, and was obedient to them. His mother treasured all these things in her heart. And Jesus increased in wisdom and in years, and in divine and human favor.

LUKE 2:51–52

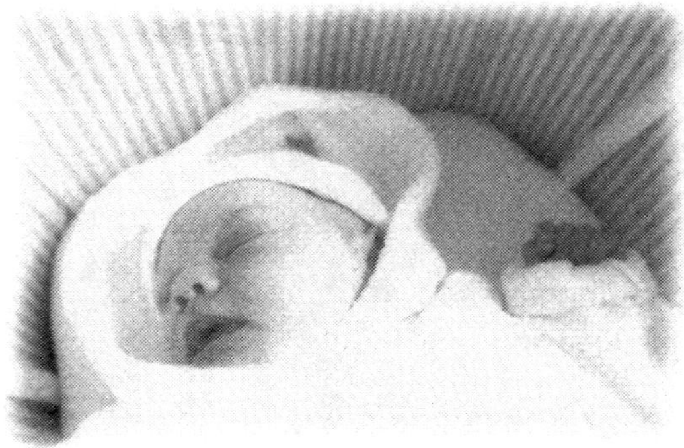

Blessing for a Crib or Cradle or the New Baby's Room/Nursery

God of all places and times,
bless this place where my child will sleep.
May it be a safe haven,
with peaceful dreams and much joy,
filled with lullabies, prayers, and comforting stories.

Send your angels to watch over this place
so that it may witness much wonder
and the gradual discovery of this amazing world
that you have given us for our delight.

Help my child to rest well here,
secure in both my love and in yours.
Amen

> ***While they were there, the time came for her [Mary] to deliver her child. And she gave birth to her firstborn son. . . and laid him in a manger, because there was no place for them at the inn.***
>
> **LUKE 2:6–7**

Blessing for the New Grandparents

God of all generations,
please bless these new grandparents
who now delight in their grandchild.

Help them to see how much their love is like yours,
a love which also delights in us just as we are.
Help them to be faithful reflections of that love,
patient and ready to support and help the parents
whenever they are needed.

(Those present may trace the sign of the cross on the grandparents' foreheads.)

Thank you for all the ways that we see your love
reflected in their faithful love for others.
We ask you to bless them
in the name of the Father, and of the Son, and of the Holy Spirit.
Amen

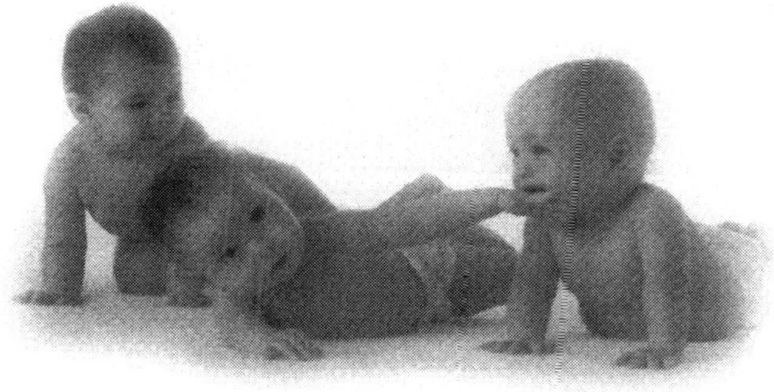

This is my covenant with them, says the LORD: my spirit that is upon you, and my words that I have put in your mouth, shall not depart out of your mouth, or out of the mouths of your children, or our of the mouths of your children's children, says the LORD, from now on and forever.

ISAIAH 59:21

Blessing for the New Baby's Sibling(s)

God of love,
we ask your blessing today
on our new baby's big brother(s) and sister(s).
This new baby has already heard their voices
even before she was born,
and now she can enjoy them fully.

Help them to know that they have a big job—
and a big privilege—
to help show her how to act and how to love you.
Help them also to know that you will give them
all the graces they need to do this well.

Help us all to remember
that with another child in our family,
there is not *less* love to go around but *more,*
and that we're counting on them to help us
love her well.

(Those present may trace the sign of the cross on the child's forehead.)

Bless this big sister (and brother)
in the name of the Father, and of the Son, and of the Holy Spirit.
Amen

> ***He [Jesus] called a child, whom he put among them, and said, "Truly I tell you, unless you change and become like children, you will never enter the kingdom of heaven. Whoever becomes humble like this child is the greatest in the kingdom of heaven."***
>
> **MATTHEW 18:2–4**

Blessing for the New Baby's Stepsibling(s)

Loving Mother and Father of us all,
please bless the brother of our new baby.
Although these two may not share both parents,
they share our love and the opportunity
to make this family a place of love and acceptance.

Help this big brother to know
that with another child in our family
there is not *less* love to go around but *more,*
and that we're counting on him
to help us love our new baby well.

*(Those present may trace the sign of the cross
on the child's forehead.)*

Bless this wonderful big brother
in the name of the Father, and of the Son, and of the Holy Spirit.
Amen

> ***And pointing to his disciples, he [Jesus] said, "Here are my mother and my brothers! For whoever does the will of my Father in heaven is my brother and sister and mother."***
>
> **MATTHEW 12:49–50**

For the First Few Days and Weeks

And the one who was seated on the throne said, "See, I am making all things new."
Revelation 21:5

God of all beginnings,
we are still getting used to life with our new baby.
Give us patience as we cope with so many new challenges—
often with less sleep than in the past.

Help us to remember
that this time will not last all that long
and that you are in our midst—
especially when we are least aware of it—
helping shape us into parents and into a family,
with ties that are deeper than we can describe
or even imagine.

Help us to know your whispered presence
in all the new experiences and the learning
that is part of this time,
and in the amazing new life that we see before us.
Keep us open to hearing your voice and seeing your presence,
especially where we may least expect it.
Amen

On the Baby Waking

Loving God, just now I hear the baby waking up.
I had hoped that she might sleep a little longer—
to give her more rest and me more of a break.
But her cries remind me of what a miracle it is
that she is healthy and that she has the gift of life
and is even able to make the sounds I now hear.

As I go to greet her,
help me to show her how special she is,
and to look with fresh eyes at her,
and at all the ways that she so obviously needs me
and is always exploring and learning new things.
Give me the gift of seeing her
with just a bit of the wonder and love
with which you look at each of us
every minute of our lives.

Help me to give her all that she needs
to understand your love through my love for her.
Amen

Awake, O harp and lyre!
I will awake the dawn.
I will give thanks to you,
O Lord, among the peoples,
and I will sing praises to
you among the nations.
For your steadfast love is
higher than the heavens,
and your faithfulness
reaches to the clouds.
Psalm 108:2–4

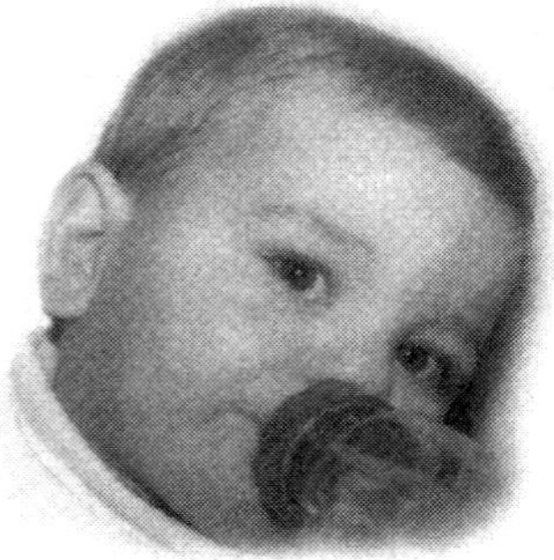

While Nursing or Feeding the Newborn

Nourishing God,
thank you for the privilege of this time
to feed my child,
a time to put other demands "on hold"
and to just focus on our relationship.

Although I am the one feeding him,
when I pause and think about it,
he is also "nourishing" me—
by giving me the opportunity to give to him
and to realize all that I am able to give.
And he can also teach me about your love
because my relationship to *you* is much like
his relationship to *me:*
You delight to "feed" me whenever I ask,
and you want me to know your love
through all that you give me.

As I feed my child, help me to be grateful
for the ability to give him what he needs when he needs it;
please be with those parents throughout the world
who aren't able to give their children all that they need,
even though they want to.
Amen

Rejoice with Jerusalem, and be glad for her,
all you who love her;
rejoice with her in joy,
all you who mourn over her—
that you may nurse and be satisfied
from her consoling breast;
that you may drink deeply with delight
from her glorious bosom.

Isaiah 66:10–11

For the Challenges of Breast-Feeding

Tender, gracious God,
I'm not doing too well at breast-feeding this child right now.
We can't seem able to get this nursing relationship
going the way I had hoped.

Help me to remember that I need to be patient
and that I may need to seek some help,
but also that the biggest need is for me to *relax,*
so that I can help both of us to do that.

Help me to take care of myself,
getting the rest and the fluids that I need,
and to remember that you have built my body
to give this little one just what he needs.
Help me to see this time as a prayer
and a way to appreciate how you nurture me
while I am nurturing him.

Help me to treasure this time together—
however I end up feeding him—
a time to give him the food that he needs
but also to give him the love and nurture
that helps us both blossom and bond in a very special way.

Thank you for giving me the ability
to nurture my child in this wonderful way;
be with us both to help us to relax and just enjoy each other,
while both of us are held in your love.
Amen

Rid yourselves of all…envy….Like newborn infants, long for the pure, spiritual milk, so that by it you may grow into salvation—if indeed you have tasted that the Lord is good.

1 Peter 2:1–3

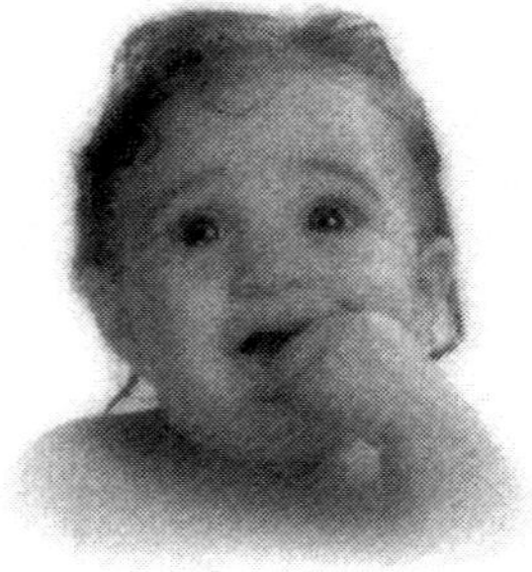

While Changing the New Baby's Diapers

Dear God of all creation,
it's time to change the baby's diapers.
While the task itself may not be all that attractive,
this gives me time just to focus on her and her tiny body.

Help me to appreciate
how amazing and intricate her body is,
while its ability to take the nourishment she receives
and change it into just what she needs,
so that she can continue to grow and change
and to keep discovering this fascinating world around her
and never to be ashamed of it or to wish it were different.

And help me to keep her safe—
no matter what she is doing—
and to take the time to talk and play with her.

Then she can begin to appreciate
how important it is to just enjoy life,
and she can also know what an amazing
little person she is.

Thank you for this time with her—
even to change a wet or smelly diaper.
Amen

I am also mortal, like everyone else,
a descendant of the first-formed child of earth;
and in the womb of a mother
I was molded into flesh. . . .
And when I was born, I began to breathe
the common air,
and fell upon the kindred earth;
my first sound was a cry, as is true of all.
I was nursed with care in swaddling cloths.

Wisdom 7:1, 3–4

Evening Prayer While Tucking in a Newborn

God of our days and nights,
please bless this little one
as he rests in your care throughout this night.

Keep him safe in your love and in ours;
give him good dreams,
and after a peaceful night,
give him the energy and the gifts he needs tomorrow
to be and do all that you have made him to be.

(Parents may trace a cross on the infant's forehead.)

Bless him in the name of the Father, and of the Son, and of the Holy Spirit.
Amen

When you lie down, sleep will be sweet.
Do not be afraid.
Proverbs 3:24–25

On Going to the Doctor's Office

Loving God,
we are here to see the doctor
for a check-up and a shot for the baby.
Although it can seem like a lot of work
for us to get here,
we are very fortunate to be able to
check on his health.

Please give the doctor and nurse
all the wisdom and expertise they need
to help my child
and to respond to any questions or concerns
I may have.

Thank you for his good health
and for the opportunity for such good healthcare
for my child.

Please bless all those children and parents
who do not have such resources in their lives.

Keep my child healthy and happy,
growing and thriving in your love and mine.
Help him to always take good care of his health
and to have access to the resources to do so.

Thank you for all the ways that you take care of us
with tender, gentle care.
Amen

Honor physicians for their services,
for the Lord created them;
for their gift of healing comes from the Most High. . . .
The skill of the physicians makes them distinguished,
and in the presence of the great they are admired.

SIRACH 38:1–3

Prayer About Having Little Time

God of all my days,
where has the time gone lately?
About the time I start to do something
it seems that there are several interruptions,
and I may not get back to what I started
until much later that day, if then.

Help me to be aware that,
in the midst of all the unexpected demands
with a small child,
this is time for me to practice
being in the moment.

Give me the grace of flexibility
and help me begin to see you more clearly
in the midst of the interruptions—

where you are to be found
when I look more carefully—
because I just can't plan very far at all most days.

Thank you for all your patience with me;
help me to be more patient with myself
and with the many demands on my time lately—
even when those demands feel difficult.
Amen

For [God] says:
"At an acceptable time I have listened to you,
and on a day of salvation I have helped you."

See, now is the acceptable time; see, now is the day of salvation!

2 CORINTHIANS 6:2

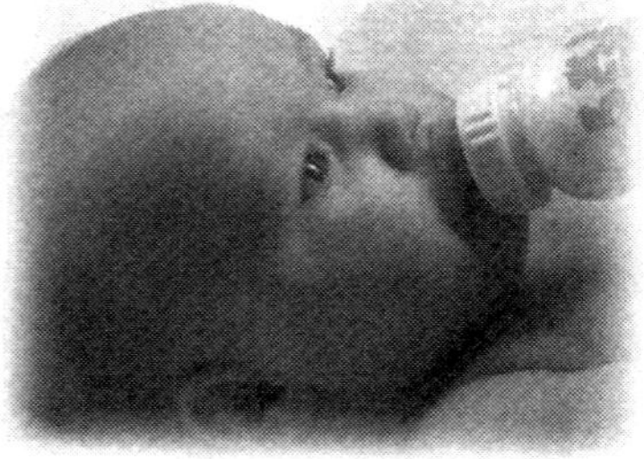

Prayer During a Night Feeding

God of my days and nights,
here we are, in the middle of the night:
you, my child, and I.

Help me to use this time
as I comfort and feed my baby
as a special time of prayer and reflection,
just to be with you.

Thank you for the aspects of life
which seem clearer at night—
for the moon and the stars and the wonder of space,
and for a safe place to live,
which I can so easily take for granted.
Thank you, too, for all those who are working tonight
so that the rest of us can sleep well.

Keep this child—and all the children of the world—
safe and healthy this night.
Help them to come to know your love
through the love they experience in their lives.

Help me also to remember how tenderly you hold *me*
as I now hold this child, hungry for milk and for love.

When this child is satisfied,
help us both get back to sleep,
so that we can greet the morning,
refreshed and ready to experience the gifts
that you have waiting for us tomorrow.
Amen

"Bless the Lord, nights and days;
sing praise to him and highly exalt him forever."
DANIEL 3:71

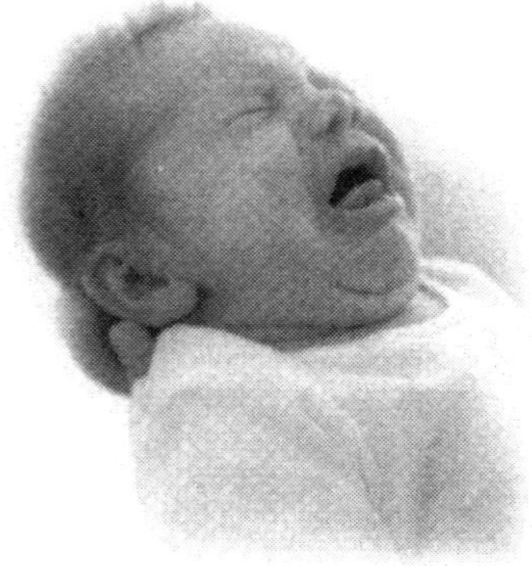

A Meditation for a Fussy Baby

(You may want to say this aloud rhythmically as you're rocking or walking with a fussy infant.)

Loving God, please be with this child,
be with this child, be with this child.

Our God loves you—just as you are,
just as you are, just as you are.

And I love you—just as you are,
just as you are, just as you are.

Dear God, give us the grace that we need,
the grace that we need, the grace that we need.

Loving God, please hold us in love,
hold us in love, hold us in love.
Amen

[God says:]
"I led them with cords of human kindness,
with bands of love.
I was to them like those
who lift infants to their cheeks.
I bent down to them and fed them.
HOSEA 11:4

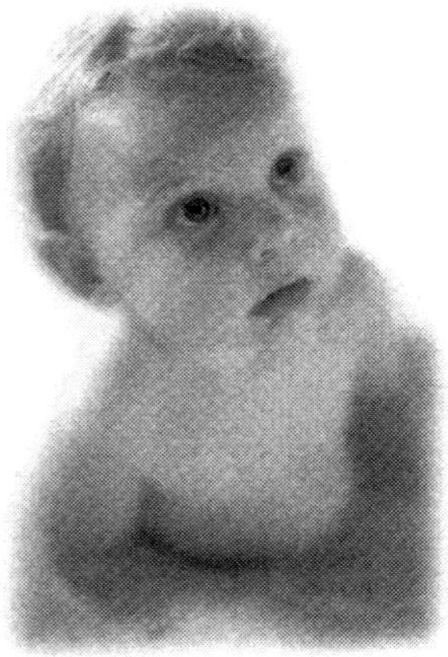

After Bathing the New Baby

God of all rivers, streams, and oceans,
thank you for the gift of water
and for this time for our child
to experience the wonder of it.

Thank you for the opportunity to enjoy
the whole process of a bath with her:
taking off her clothes and entering the water,
splashing around in it and soaping up and rinsing off,
and then wrapping her up in a warm, soft towel.

Thank you for all our senses,
which are so powerfully involved in this experience,
and thank you for this little person
who helps us to see all this with new eyes.

Bless *all* her baths and showers,
her swimming, and other adventures with water.

Keep her safe near water
and help her to know that
her body is wonderful
and never anything to be ashamed of.

Thank you for the opportunity
to renew our sense of wonder
as we bathe this child.
Amen

Then he [Jesus] poured water into a basin and began to wash the disciples' feet and to wipe them with the towel that was tied around him.
JOHN 13:5

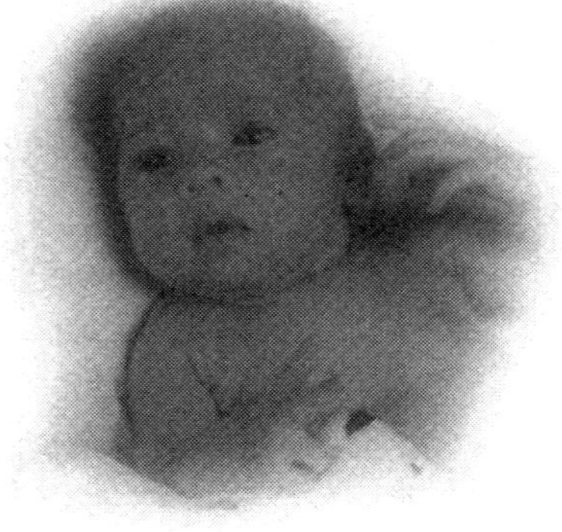

Massaging the New Baby

Loving and tender God,
thank you for this little one before me
and the opportunity to touch him in a gentle way.

You made us in your image and likeness
and covered us with skin, this amazing gift,
through which we have so many sensations
and so much information.

Thank you for our skin and the sense of touch—
and for all our senses, which help us to learn
so much about you and all that you have created.

As I rub and touch my little one,
help my fingers to show him
how much I love him and how special he is.
Help me—and all the people he will meet in his life—
to always touch him lovingly and never harshly.

Help him to always be tender, in turn,
in the way he touches and treats others.
Help him to use every part of this body as he grows
to care for and serve others.

Thank you for the gift of this time with him
to just enjoy the sense of touch.
Amen

And all in the crowd were trying to touch him [Jesus], for power came out from him and healed all of them.
LUKE 6:19

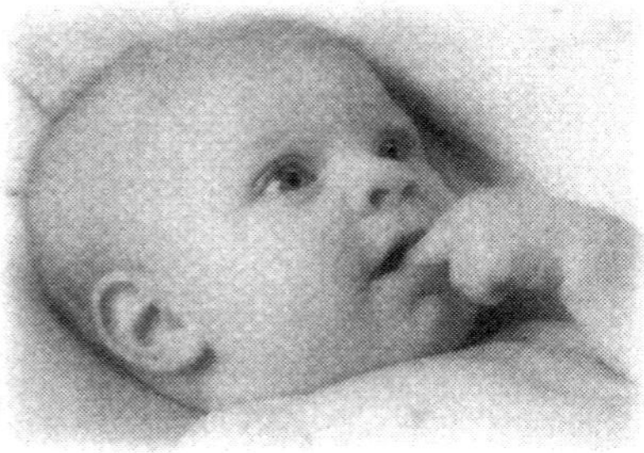

Thanksgiving for the Baby's First Smile

Laughing God, it finally happened.
After what seems like a long time of feeding
and holding and changing and bathing this child,
there it was: the first smile.

How could I have imagined how precious
that smile would be?
Is this a hint of how precious it is
when *I* finally turn to you
after you have lavished so much love on *me*?

Please help this to be the first of many smiles,
of much laughter and joy in this child's life,
joy at this wonderful world you have given us
for our delight.

Help me to remember this smile, and others like it,
when it feels like no one notices all that I do for this baby.
Help me to remember how important I am to this child
and that you see all that I do for this little one.
And remind me that your delight in me
may look very much like the wonderful smile that I just saw.
Amen

In your presence there is fullness of joy;
in your right hand are pleasures forevermore.
PSALM 16:11

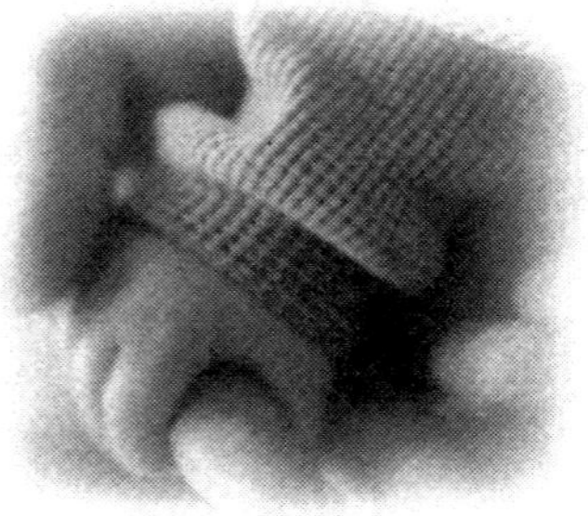

Leaving the Baby With a Sitter or at Day Care

Tender God,
it isn't easy to leave my child with someone else;
it's hard not knowing how the baby will respond
when I'm not here.

Help me to trust in the sitter's love and care
—and in yours—when I'm not there.
This separation is only one of so many
that we will have in our lives,
and each time a little of my heart is left behind.
But help us both to learn that love doesn't know distance
and that our love can be present for each other,
even when I am away.

Thank you for this sitter;
give her the graces and wisdom she needs
to care well for my child while I am gone,
and help her to appreciate the trust I put in her.

Bless all those children who are left in another's care;
bring them safely back to their parents,
knowing that a whole community cares for them.
And help us all to remember
how tenderly we are held in your care.
Amen

For you, O Lord, are my hope,
my trust, O LORD, from my youth.
Upon you I have leaned since birth;
it was you who took me from my mother's womb.
My praise is continually of you.
PSALM 71:5

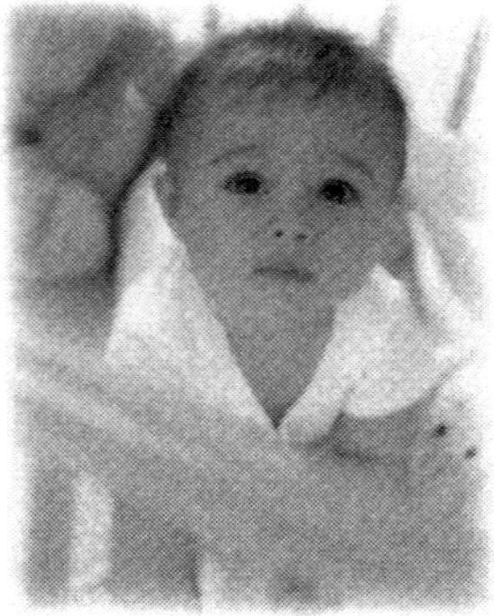

Blessing for the New Baby's First Toys

God of all play and all delights,
please bless these toys
and all the others that our little one will enjoy
and delight in throughout the years.

Help these toys to guide her exploration of the world
and help her to appreciate the wonder and vastness
of all that you have created.

Keep her safe as she plays;
help her learn to share
and to pick them up when the time comes.
Help us to remember that she is never more like you
than when she is playing and delighting in life.
Help us to take time to play with her
and to learn again from her how to play.

Give us wisdom in giving her the toys
that will best help her to grow
and to become the person you have created her to be.
Amen

[Wisdom speaks:]
"When he [God] established the heavens I was there,
when he drew a circle on the face of the deep,
when he made firm the skies above,
when he established the fountains of the deep,
when he assigned to the sea its limit,
so that the waters might not transgress his command;
when he marked out the foundations of the earth,
then I was beside him, like a master worker;
and I was daily his delight,
rejoicing before him always,
rejoicing in his inhabited world
and delighting in the human race.
PROVERBS 8:27–31

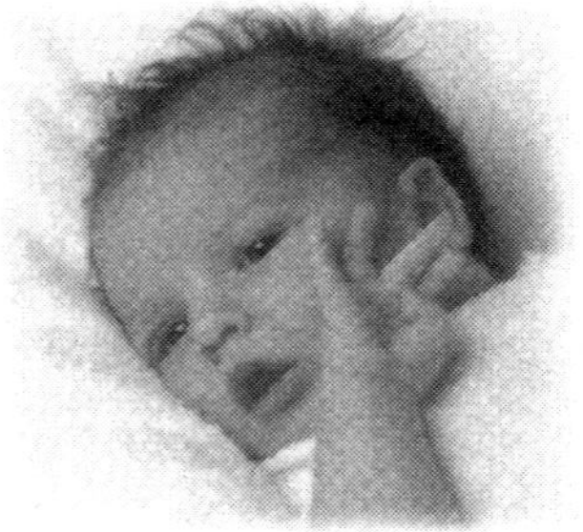

On the New Baby's Baptism

Loving God,
thank you for the opportunity to celebrate baptism
with our child and our friends and families.
Help us to be able to look beyond all the details of the day
to see that you are calling both our child and us
to a deeper life of faith.

Thank you for the faith community of our parish,
that welcomes our child on behalf of the whole Church.
Help them and us to teach our child
what it means to believe in you—
both by who we are and by what we say.

Give us the gifts to teach this child about faith.
Help us remember that our family is the first experience
of the community of believers that we call "church"
that our child will know.
Be present in our "domestic church"
and in our hospitality to those who come into our home.

As our child was baptized
into your death and resurrection,
help us to be willing to "die and rise" with you—
day in and day out—as we care for this child.

Continue to teach us through this child
and through our love for him
about yourself and your amazing, patient love for us.
Amen

Guided by the Spirit, Simeon came into the temple; and when the parents brought in the child Jesus, to do for him what was customary under the law, Simeon took him in his arms and praised God, saying,

***"Master, now you are dismissing your servant in peace,
according to your word;
for my eyes have seen your salvation,
which you have prepared in the presence of all peoples,
a light for revelation to the Gentiles, and glory to your people Israel."***

LUKE 2:27–32

On Having Solid Food for the First Time

Loving God,
our child is now ready for more than just
milk and juice.

It seems that just yesterday she was a newborn,
needing to be held and waiting for milk.
Now here she sits, ready to try this interesting food
that the rest of us have been eating.

She has no idea of the amazing range
of flavors and spices which await her tongue—
just as she has no idea of all the experiences
which await her in the years to come.

Help her to "savor"
all that she comes to know in her life
and to use food and other good things
in moderation and with respect.

Give her always enough to eat
and help her, in her own way,
to make the world a place where no child goes hungry.

Thank you for all the amazing ways
that she is growing and changing.
Amen

O taste and see that the LORD is good;
happy are those who take refuge in him.
PSALM 34:8

On the Baby Outgrowing Clothes

God of all growing things,
here is proof that my baby is growing and changing:
he no longer fits into these clothes
that used to fit him easily.

Although there is a part of me
that is eager to see him grow and change,
there is also a part of me that would like him
to stay little, just the way he is—or has been.

Help me to be open to all the new possibilities
that this child will lead me to as he grows:
new interests, hobbies, sports, even to adolescence.
Give me the grace to appreciate the present moment as a parent,
knowing that before long it will change
and a new challenge will present itself.

Thank you for the time to enjoy my little one
as an infant;
help me to savor these days that are quickly passing.
Amen

> ***But each of us was given grace according to the measure of Christ's gift... until all of us come to the unity of faith and of the knowledge of the Son of God, to maturity, to the measure of the full stature of Christ.***
>
> **EPHESIANS 4:7, 13–16**

On the Child Beginning to Crawl or Walk

God of all places,
our child is on the move!
Suddenly our home is starting to change
as we need to put things out of reach and
block off spaces
that we didn't need to worry about before.

It's wonderful to see our daughter grow and change,
but it also makes life a bit more complicated.
Help us to rejoice in her freedom—
as you do for each of us—
and help us not to worry about the changes
this may mean.

Our little one has been leaving us
since the moment she was born,
and she will continue to do so in more and more ways
as the years go by.

Help us to let her go—as you let us go—
while still guiding her in appropriate ways.
Thank you for the wonder of all that she can do,
which seems to be more amazing
with every passing week or month.
Keep her safe and healthy in her newfound mobility.
Amen

When Israel was a child, I loved him,
and out of Egypt I called my son.
The more I called them,
the more they went from me. . . .
Yet it was I who taught Ephraim to walk,
I took them up in my arms.

Hosea 11:1–3

On the Child's First Birthday

God of all time,
can it be?
Can he really be one year old already?

It really doesn't seem possible that so much
could have all been crowded into the past year:
the labor and birth, the first few nights and days
and so much since then.
The tiny little one who mostly slept
has become the charmer who smiles
and not only rolls over but sits up, crawls, and stands.

How can you have accomplished all this—
plus all that he has learned—in one year?
Meanwhile you have been shaping us
as parents and as a family
into the right place for this little one
to continue to grow and to thrive.
You truly are an amazing God.

Please continue to give us the graces
that we will need
in this coming year to help our son
continue to blossom;
keep him safe and help him continue to grow
in an awareness of our love and yours.
And give us a sense of wonder at all the ways
that you are at work in his life.
Amen

The child [Jesus] grew and became strong, filled with wisdom; and the favor of God was upon him.
LUKE 2:40

Our Favorite Prayers for Babies

Our Favorite Prayers for Babies